THE A.B.C.
of
PIANO PLAYING

An Easy Method for Beginners

by

Boris Berlin

Book One

Revised Edition
Including Elementary Technic for Beginners

New Illustrations by Carole Precious

Technical Illustrations by Acorn Technical Art Studio Inc.

ISBN 0-88797-182-2

PREFACE

The A.B.C. Piano Book has been prepared to meet the ever growing demand for a simple, yet progressive beginners' book for children.

The material in this book has been divided into lessons, thus simplifing the assignment task of the teacher, who can ask the pupils to simply learn "lesson-so-and-so for the next time". As some pupils are naturally more capable than others, the teacher will have to use discretion in presenting a lesson or giving an assignment.

Children expect to play the piano right from the beginning. Each lesson therefore contains simple tunes which the pupil can play while learning something about the keyboard and about notation. The Lessons in Writing correspond to the Lessons in Playing. They will prove invaluable as a "theory aid" in learning the pieces.

Most of the illustrations in this book relate to material presented in the corresponding lessons. The illustration in the 1st Lesson, for example, will help the student to find the groups of 2 and of 3 black keys; that in the 3rd Lesson shows the ascending and descending 2-note patterns; those in the 4th and 5th Lessons show the direction of the notes and the shape of the melody, and so on.

Elementary Technic For Beginners, which includes some useful exercises, will be found at the end of the book.

As the A.B.C. Piano Book is not meant to be self-instructing, the presentation of its contents is left to the teacher.

FOR REFERENCE

THE KEYBOARD

Note that the black keys are grouped in Twos and Threes.

Seven letters of the alphabet are used as the names of notes.
They run from left to right on the keyboard, and are repeated over and over again.

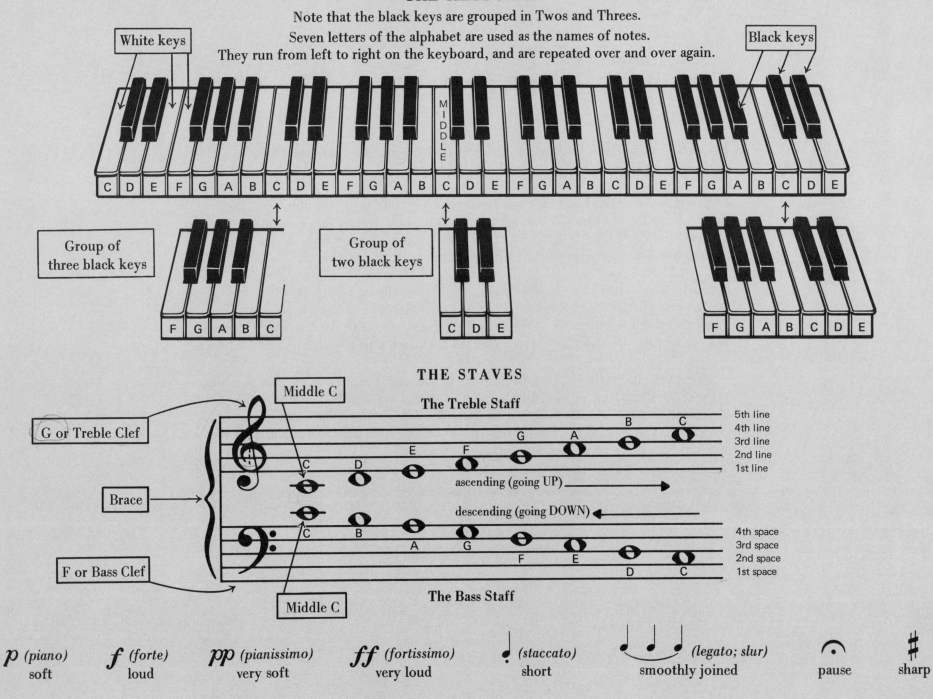

THE STAVES

The Treble Staff

The Bass Staff

p *(piano)* soft f *(forte)* loud pp *(pianissimo)* very soft ff *(fortissimo)* very loud $\dot{\rule{0pt}{1ex}}$ *(staccato)* short   *(legato; slur)* smoothly joined   pause $\sharp$ sharp

FOR REFERENCE

TIME VALUES

𝅝   Whole Note (4 beats)
(Tah - ah - ah - ah)

𝅗𝅥.   Dotted Half Note (3 beats)
(Tah - ah - ah)

𝅗𝅥   Half Note (2 beats)
(Tah - ah)

♩   Quarter Note (1 beat)
(Tah)

♫   Two Eighth Notes (1/2 beat each, two notes to 1 beat)
(Ti - ti)

NOTES AND RESTS

Whole (4 beats)   Dotted Half (3 beats)   Half (2 beats)   Quarter (1 beat)   Eighth (1/2 beat)

FINGERING

LEFT HAND   RIGHT HAND

TIME SIGNATURES

The upper figure shows the number of beats to a measure.

$\frac{2}{4}$ $\frac{3}{4}$ $\frac{4}{4}$

The lower figure shows the kind of note to one beat. (The figure 4 represents a quarter note.)

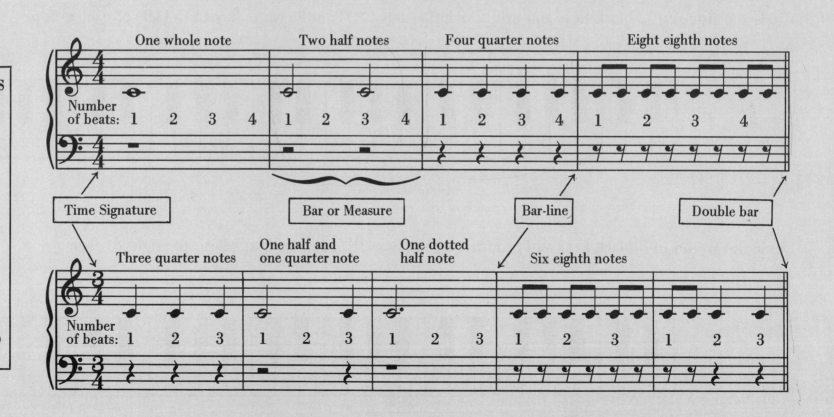

One whole note   Two half notes   Four quarter notes   Eight eighth notes

Number of beats: 1 2 3 4   1 2 3 4   1 2 3 4   1 2 3 4

Time Signature   Bar or Measure   Bar-line   Double bar

Three quarter notes   One half and one quarter note   One dotted half note   Six eighth notes

Number of beats: 1 2 3   1 2 3   1 2 3   1 2 3   1 2 3

1. Blacken the black keys.

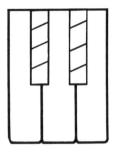
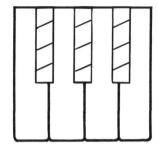

This is a group of 2 black keys.

This is a group of 3 black keys.

2. Circle the groups of 2 black keys and print the letter-name "C" on the white key to the left of each group.

3. Circle the groups of 3 black keys and print the letter-name "B" on the white key to the right of each group.

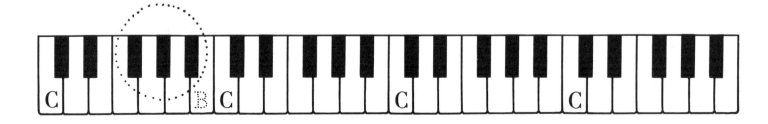

Date . . . .

Two Black Key Tunes

Play in clusters (all keys at once) all the groups of 2 BLACK KEYS.
Start on your LEFT and go UP the keyboard.————————▶
Then start on your RIGHT and go DOWN the keyboard.◀————————

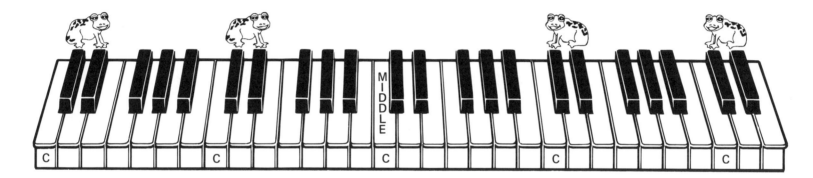

Play in clusters all the groups of 3 BLACK KEYS.
Start on your LEFT and go UP the keyboard.————————▶
Then start on your RIGHT and go DOWN the keyboard.◀————————

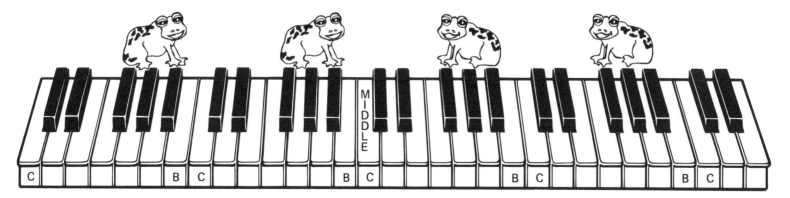

1. (a) Number the 5 lines of each staff.
   (b) Number the 4 spaces of each staff.
   (c) Trace the Middle C's.

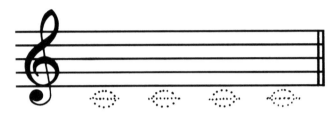
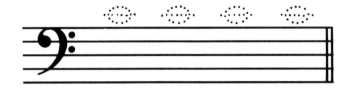

2. Draw a line through 1 block for a SHORT (1-beat) note.

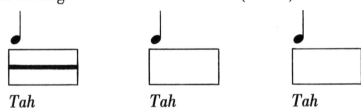
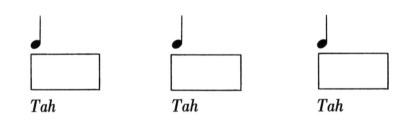

     Tah   *Tah*   *Tah*   *Tah*   *Tah*   *Tah*

3. Draw a line through 2 blocks for a LONG (2-beat) note.

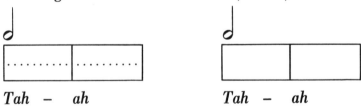
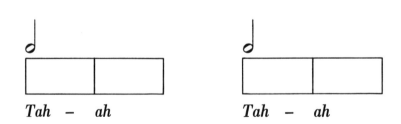

   Tah – ah   *Tah – ah*   *Tah – ah*   *Tah – ah*

4. Print letter-names on three WHITE keys:

         (a) moving DOWN from C.   (b) moving UP from C.

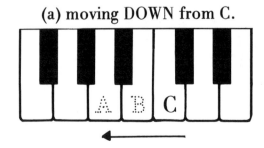
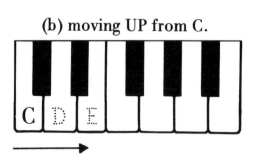

Date ....

Two Rhythm Tunes

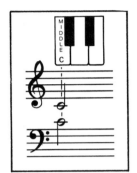

Play on Middle C saying "Short" or *"Tah"* for ♩ notes and "Long" or *"Tah-ah"* for ♪ notes.

G or Treble Clef

F or Bass Clef

Play with Right Hand:

Say: Short, Short, Long, Long, Short, Short, Long, Long.
Tah, Tah, Tah-ah, Tah-ah, Tah, Tah, Tah-ah, Tah-ah.

Play with Left Hand:

Say: Long, Short, Short, Long, Short, Short, Long, Long.
Tah-ah, Tah, Tah, Tah-ah, Tah, Tah, Tah-ah, Tah-ah.

My First Tune

Play with Right Hand:

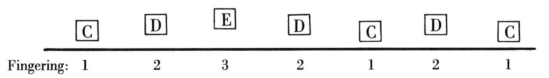

Fingering: 1 2 3 2 1 2 1

My Second Tune

Play with Left Hand:

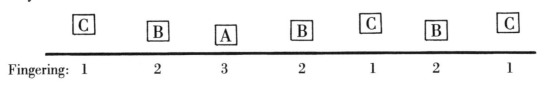

Fingering: 1 2 3 2 1 2 1

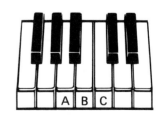

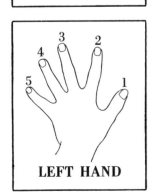

RIGHT HAND

LEFT HAND

1. Trace the notes under these pictures of the piano keyboard, then print the correct letter-name under each note.

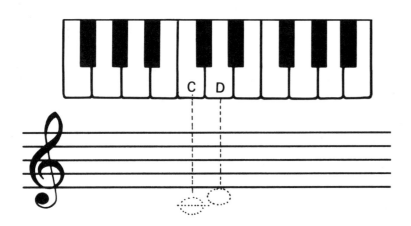 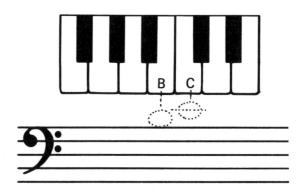

2. Draw arrows pointing UP for every 2-note pattern (C and D), then print the correct letter-name under each note.

Letter-names: C   D

3. Draw arrows pointing DOWN for every 2-note pattern (C and B), then print the correct letter-name under each note.

Letter-names: C   B

Can you find these patterns when playing "Forward" and "Down The Hill"?

Date . . . .

3rd LESSON

Two-four
time
2
4
two beats in
a measure

Fingering: └ 2 1 ┘└ 1 2 ┘
left hand   right hand

♩ Quarter note
(1-beat note)

𝅗𝅥 Half note
(2-beat note)

Forward!

Play with Right Hand:

Name notes,   C   D   C   D   C   D   C
or sing: For - ward!   For - ward!   Hur - ry!   Run!

Down the Hill

Play with Left Hand:

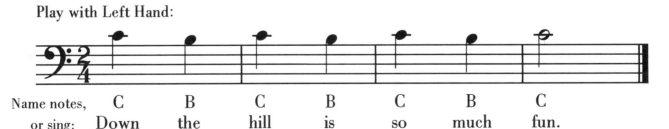

Name notes,   C   B   C   B   C   B   C
or sing: Down   the   hill   is   so   much   fun.

1. Trace the notes under these pictures of the piano keyboard, then print the correct letter-name under each note.

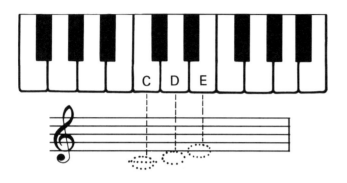
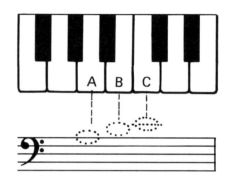

2. Draw arrows in the direction of each pattern of notes moving: (a) UP ; (b) DOWN ; (c) UP and DOWN ;

(d) DOWN and UP ; (e) repeated notes .

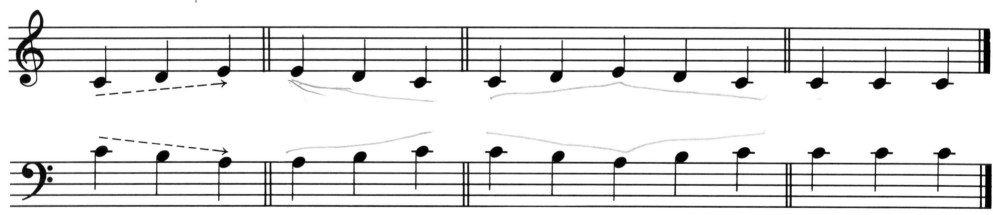

3. Write the number of beats (counts) under each note.

Number of beats: 1   2

Date . . . .

4th LESSON

Fingering: 3 2 1 | 1 2 3
left hand   right hand

The Chicks

Play with Right Hand:

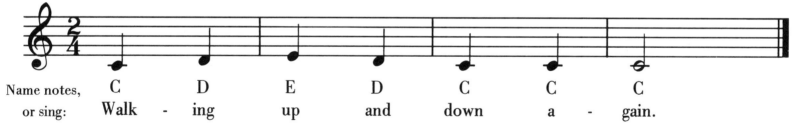

C	D	E	D	C	C	C

Name notes,
or sing: Walk - ing up and down a - gain.

The Ducklings

Play with Left Hand:

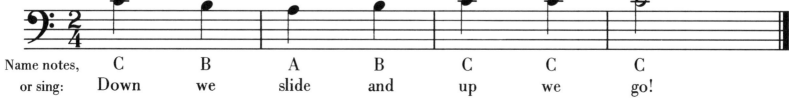

C	B	A	B	C	C	C

Name notes,
or sing: Down we slide and up we go!

1. Draw the notes under these pictures of the piano keyboard, then print the correct letter-name under each note.

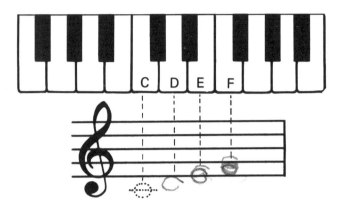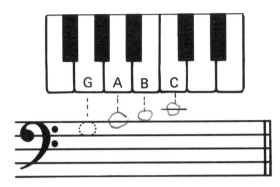

2. Trace the G (Treble) Clefs.

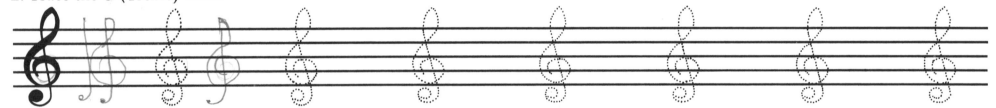

3. Draw arrows in the direction of the 7-note patterns beginning on C, then print the correct letter-name under each note.

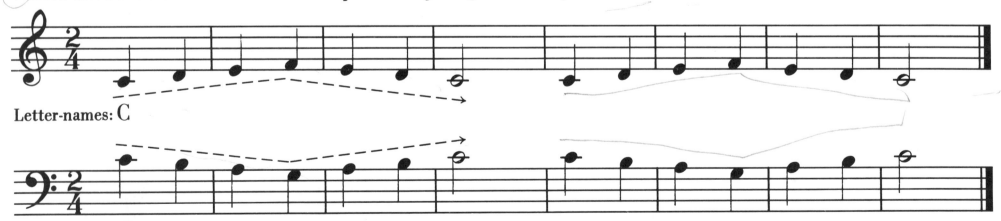

Letter-names: C

Letter-names: C

Can you find these patterns when playing "Summer Flowers" and "At The Zoo"?

Date .... *Oct 4* ....

5th LESSON

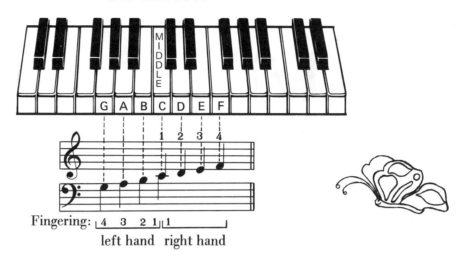

Fingering: 4 3 2 1 | 1
left hand right hand

Summer Flowers

Play with Right Hand:

Name notes, C D E F E D C C D E F E D C
or sing: Sum - mer Flow - ers smell so sweet. That is where the in - sects meet.

At The Zoo

Play with Left Hand:

Name notes, C B A G A B C C B A G A B C
or sing: Have you ev - er seen the Zoo? Mon - keys, Li - ons, Pea - cocks blue!

1. Draw the notes under these pictures of the piano keyboard, then print the correct letter-name under each note.

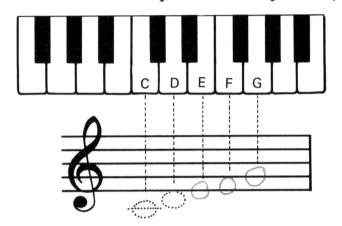 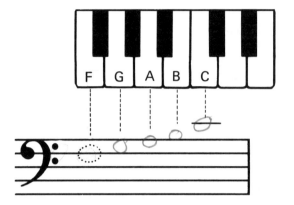

2. Fill in the blocks: 1 block for a 1-beat note, 2 blocks for a 2-beat note, and 4 blocks for a 4-beat note.

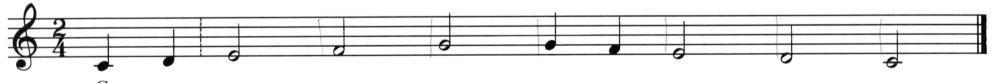

Tah   Tah-ah   Tah-ah - ah - ah   Tah-ah   Tah   Tah-ah - ah - ah   Tah-ah   Tah

3. Draw bar-lines to divide the tune into measures, then print the correct letter-name under each note.
   Add arrows in the direction of the patterns of 5 ascending and 5 descending notes.

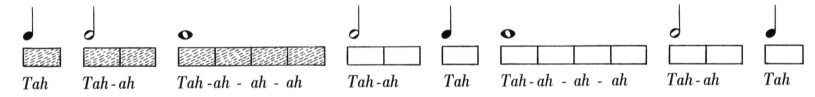

Letter-names: C

Letter-names: C

Can you find these patterns when playing "The Jolly Frog" and "The Happy Frog"?

Date .... *Oct. 4* ....

Four-four time

$$\frac{4}{4}$$

four beats in a measure

Whole note

 O

(4-beat note)

Fingering: 5 4 3 2 1 | 1
left hand | right hand

The Jolly Frog

Play with Right Hand:

Name notes, C   D   E   F   G   G   F   E   D   C
or sing: Jol - ly Frog jumps high, When he says good - bye.

The Happy Frog

Play with Left Hand:

Name notes, C   B   A   G   F   F   G   A   B   C
or sing: See the Hap - py Frog Sit - ing on a log.

Oct. 4

7th LESSON IN WRITING

1. Draw a line from each note on the staff to the corresponding key on this picture of the piano keyboard.

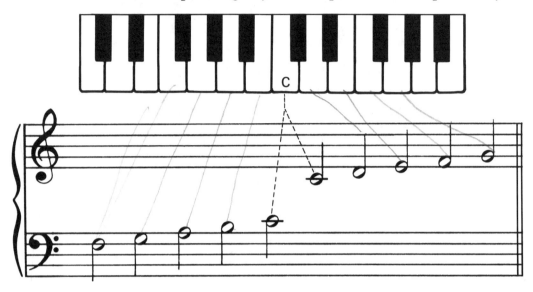

2. Trace the F (Bass) Clefs.

3. Print the correct letter-name under each note, then draw bar-lines to divide the tune into measures.
   Circle the 2-note patterns of Middle C and the note above or below it.

Letter-names: C

Can you find these patterns when playing "The Bells"?

Date .... *Oct. 4* ....

7th LESSON

The Bells

Both Hands:

Ding! Dong! Ding! Dong! Ding - ling, Ding - ling, Bells are ring - ing now!

A Rainy Day

Words by Ruth Fraser Cork

Both Hands:

Pit - ter, pat - ter rain - drops, Fresh and clear and cool,

Fall - ing on the roof - tops, Danc - ing in the pool.

Count aloud and clap the notes in each of these pieces.

Oct. 4

1. Print the correct letter-name on each key, then draw a line from each note on the staff to the corresponding key.

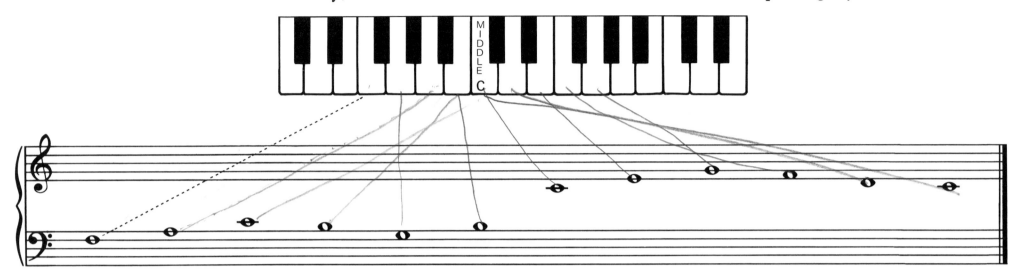

2. Write the number of beats (counts) under each note.

Number
of beats: 1   1   2   4   1   2   1   2   2   4

3. Print the correct letter-name under each note and add a time-signature at the beginning of each staff. Circle each of the four patterns found in this tune.

Letter-names: C   B   A   G   C   B   A   G

Can you find these patterns when playing "My Funny Puppy"?

Date .....Oct. 4.........

8th LESSON
My Kitty

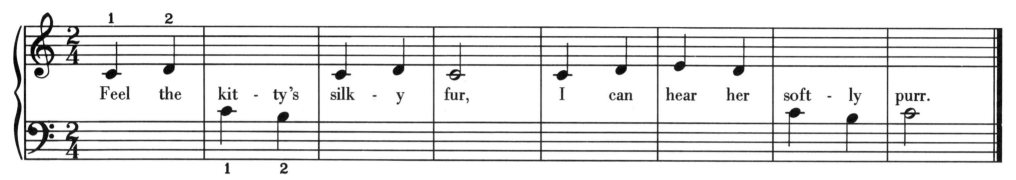

Feel the kit - ty's silk - y fur, I can hear her soft - ly purr.

Remember: $\frac{2}{4}$ Time has one strong beat (first) and one weak beat (second).

My Funny Puppy

Words by T.R.

Watch my pup - py chase the kite! He is real - ly quite a sight.

Suggestion: Play each piece three times: first singing the letter-names, then counting the beats, then singing the words.

1. Print the correct letter-name under each key marked **x**.

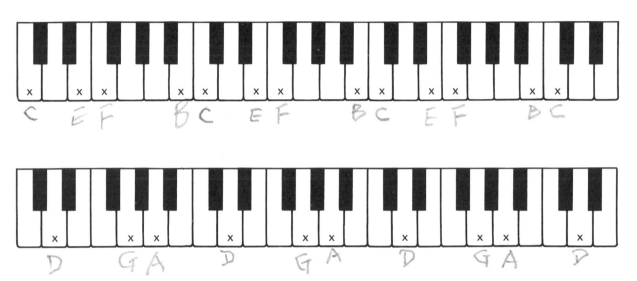

C E F B C E F B C E F B C

D G A D G A D G A D

2. Circle the correct answer.

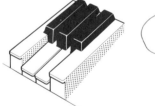

This is   (a step.)

a skip.

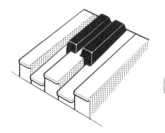

This is   a step.

(a skip.)

3. Draw notes moving by a skip of a THIRD (skipping over one white key).

Moving UP:

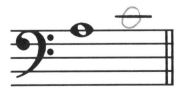

Moving DOWN:

Date ......Oct. 4...........

Summer Showers

Count aloud and clap:

E - C: a skip of a third.

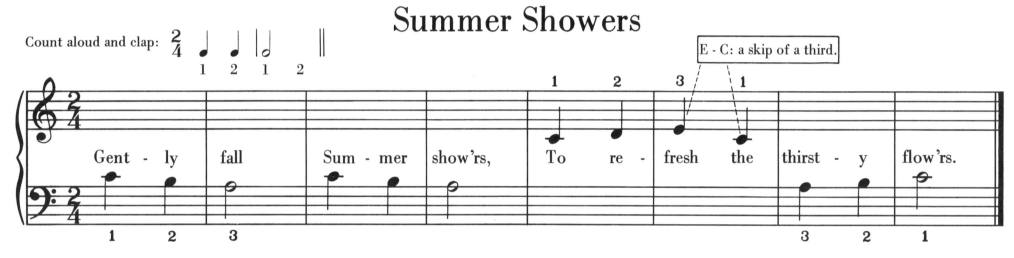

Gent - ly fall Sum - mer show'rs, To re - fresh the thirst - y flow'rs.

A Tune

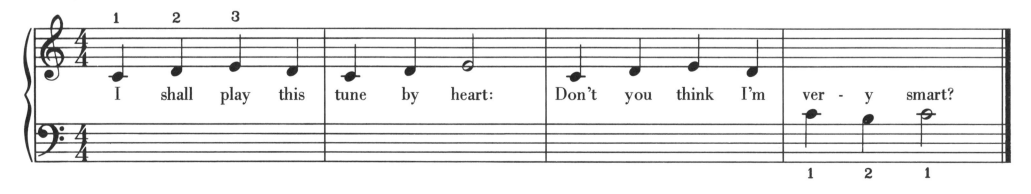

I shall play this tune by heart: Don't you think I'm ver - y smart?

Oct. 4

1. Draw a note for each letter-name.

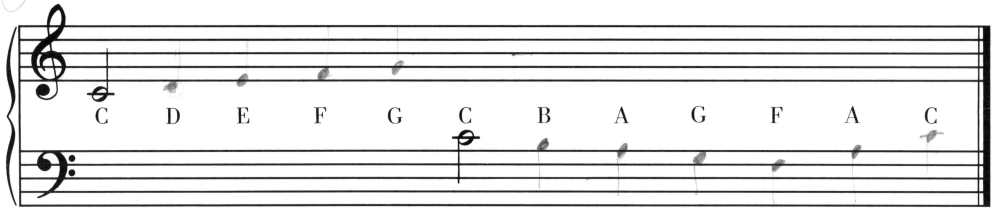

C D E F G C B A G F A C

2. Write the number of beats (counts) under each note.

Number
of beats: 1   1   2   3   1   4   3   1   1   3   4   1   3   1   4

3. Draw bar-lines to divide the tune into measures. Print the correct letter-name under each note, then add arrows in the direction of each 4-note pattern.

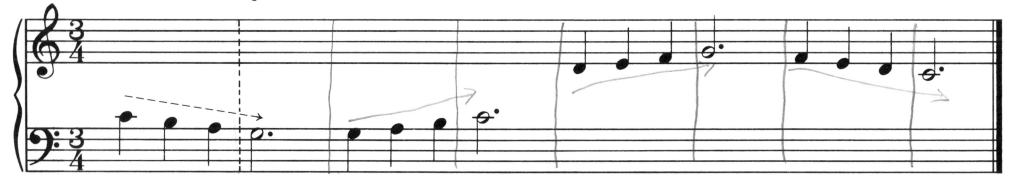

Letter-names: C

Can you find these patterns when playing "Puppy and I"?

Date .....Oct. 4.........

10th LESSON

Three-four
time

$\frac{3}{4}$

three beats in a
measure

Dotted
Half note

(3-beat note)

My Dolly

Words by Ruth Fraser Cork

Hold 3 beats: 1, 2, 3.

Sum - mer and fall, win - ter and spring, I like to play with my dol - ly, and sing.

Puppy and I

Count aloud and clap: $\frac{3}{4}$ 1 2 3 1 2 3

Words by T.R.

Pup - py and I go for a run. He chas - es sticks, we have such fun.

Remember: $\frac{3}{4}$ Time has one strong beat and two weak beats.

1. Fill in the blocks: 1 block for a 1-beat note, 2 blocks for a 2-beat note and 3 blocks for a 3-beat note.

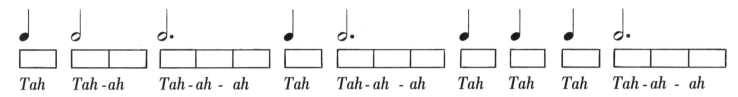

Tah   Tah - ah   Tah - ah - ah   Tah   Tah - ah - ah   Tah   Tah   Tah   Tah - ah - ah

2. Draw notes moving by a skip of a FOURTH (skipping over two white keys).

3. Draw bar-lines to divide this tune into measures. Print the correct letter-name under each note, then circle each pattern of 4 or 5 notes moving in the same direction (UP, or DOWN).

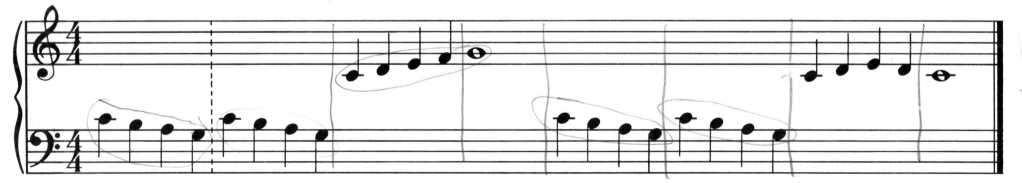

Letter-names: C B

How many patterns can you find in this tune?

Date ...... *Oct. 4* ......

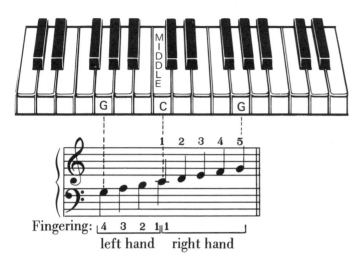

Fingering: 4 3 2 1 | 1

left hand   right hand

Mr. Moon

Words by Ruth Fraser Cork

In the sky the moon is shin - ing, Twin-kling stars are bright. Day is done, it's time to rest, So Mis-ter Moon, good night.

Apple Pie!

C - F: a fourth

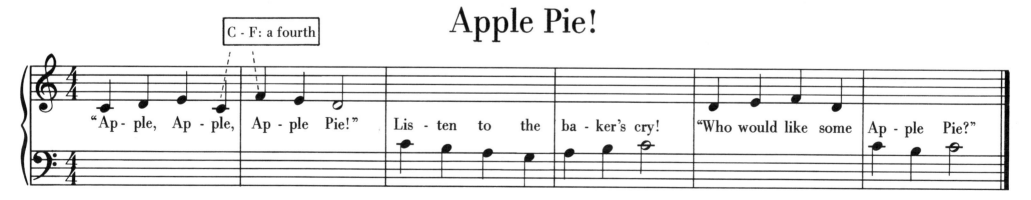

"Ap - ple, Ap - ple, Ap - ple Pie!" Lis - ten to the ba - ker's cry! "Who would like some Ap - ple Pie?"

Count aloud and clap the notes in each of these pieces.

Oct. 4

1. Draw a note for each letter-name.

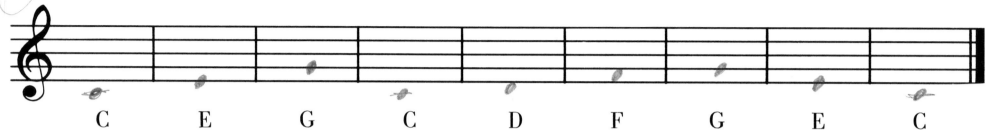

C   E   G   C   D   F   G   E   C

2. Draw a note for each letter-name.

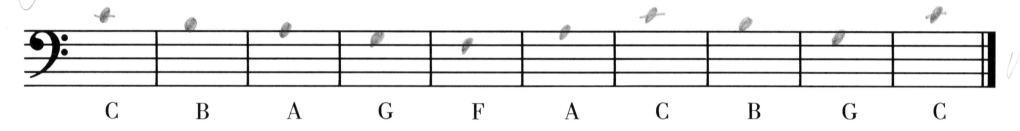

C   B   A   G   F   A   C   B   G   C

3. Draw bar-lines to divide this tune into measures, then write the number of beats (counts) under each note.

Number of beats: 2   1

Date ....Oct. 4........

A Slur

A curved line over a group of notes, indicating phrasing and a legato touch.

The Old Mill

Words by Ruth Fraser Cork

When the bus-y | mill wheel | turns a - | round, | Wa - ter splash-es | up, | falls up - on the | ground.

Peter White

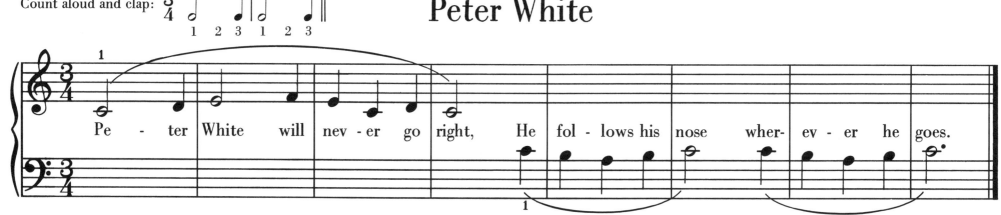

Count aloud and clap: 3/4 ♩ ♩♩ ♩ | 1 2 3 1 2 3

Pe - ter White will nev - er go right, He fol - lows his nose wher- ev - er he goes.

1. Print the correct letter-name on each of the white keys, then draw a line from each note on the staff to the BLACK key above (and to the right of) the corresponding white key.

2. Circle the correct answer.

These notes move:

UP.   DOWN.   UP and DOWN.

DOWN.   UP.   DOWN and UP.

3. Fill in the blocks: 1 block for a 1-beat note, 2 blocks for a 2-beat note, 3 blocks for a 3-beat note, 4 blocks for a 4-beat note.

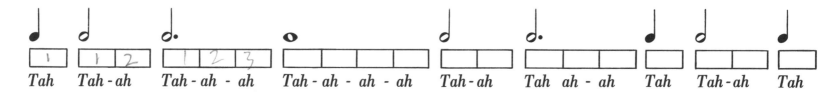

Tah   Tah - ah   Tah - ah - ah   Tah - ah - ah - ah   Tah - ah   Tah ah - ah   Tah   Tah - ah   Tah

Yankee Doodle

Yan-kee Doo-dle | went to town, a- | rid-ing on a | po - ny; | Stuck a feath-er | in his cap, and | called it Mac - a- | ro - ni.

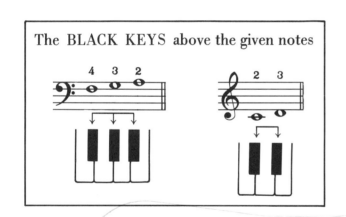

The BLACK KEYS above the given notes

A Tea Party

Play on the BLACK KEYS above the given notes.

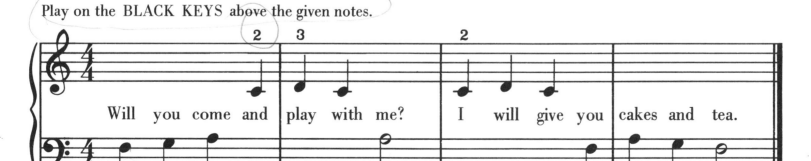

Will you come and | play with me? | I will give you | cakes and tea.

Oct. 25

1. Draw a line from each note on the staff to the corresponding key on this picture of the piano keyboard.

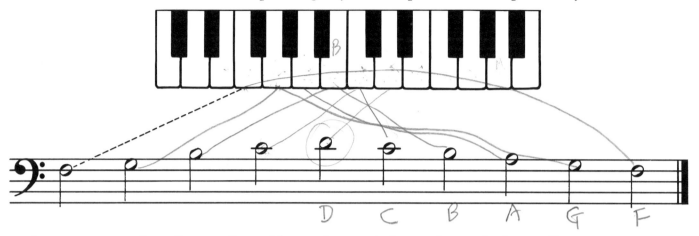

2. Draw notes whose values correspond to the number of beats (counts) shown beneath the staff.

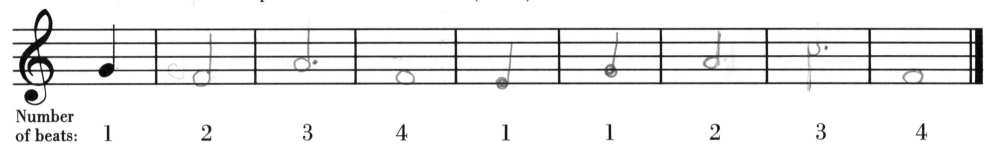

Number
of beats: 1   2   3   4   1   1   2   3   4

3. Draw a note for each letter-name, then circle each pair of notes forming a skip of a FIFTH.

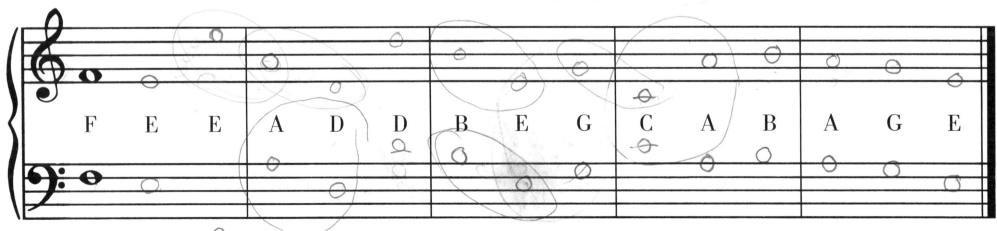

F   E   E   A   D   D   B   E   G   C   A   B   A   G   E

Date . . . . *Oct. 25., Nov 1*

14th LESSON

p (piano) soft

f (forte) loud

Fingering of the left hand

On the Bridge

Sur le pont d'Avignon,
L'on y danse, l'on y danse,
Sur le pont d'Avignon,
L'on y danse tout en rond.

G - C: a fifth

French Folk Song

p A - vig - non   has   a   bridge   Where there's danc - ing,   oh,   such   danc - ing;

f Girls   and   boys,   boys   and   girls,   Dance to - geth - er   on   the   bridge.

1. Print the correct letter-name under each note, then circle each pair of notes forming a skip of a THIRD.

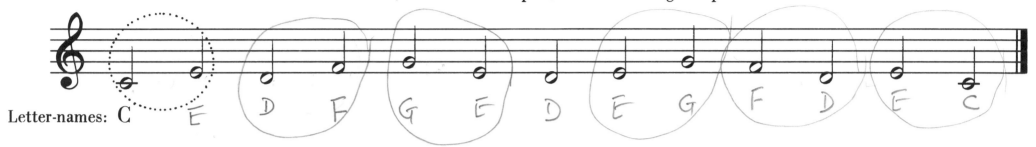

Letter-names: C   E   D   F   G   E   D   E   G   F   D   E   C

2. Print the correct letter-name under each note, then circle each pair of notes forming a skip of a FOURTH.

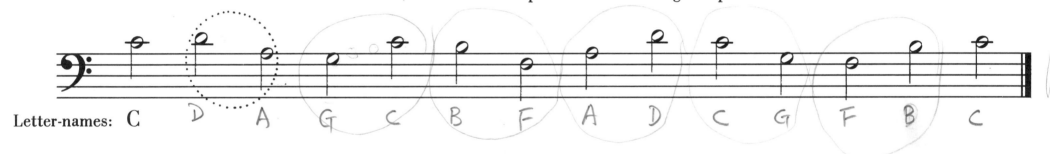

Letter-names: C   D   A   G   C   B   F   A   D   C   G   F   B   C

3. Complete each measure by adding notes, then write the number of beats (counts) under each note.

Number of beats: 3   1   1 1 1 2 1 1 3   2 1 1 2   2

Date .... *Oct. 25*

Au clair de la lune,
Mon ami Pierrot,
Prête-moi ta plume
Pour écrire un mot.

Ma chandelle est morte
Je n'ai plus de feu;
Ouvre-moi ta porte,
Pour l'amour de Dieu.

Count aloud and clap:

Pierrot

French Folk Song

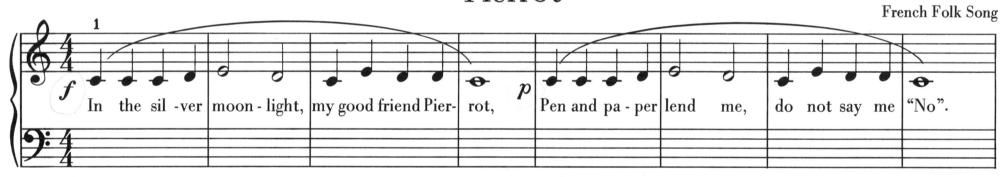

In the sil -ver moon - light, my good friend Pier- rot, Pen and pa - per lend me, do not say me "No".

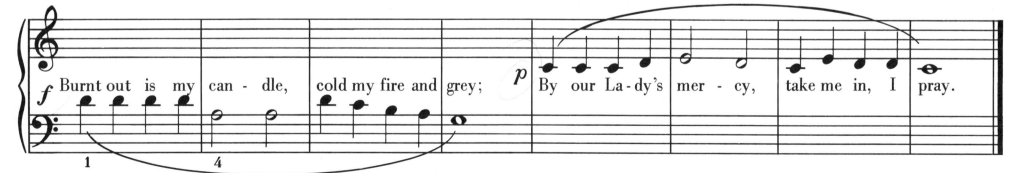

Burnt out is my can - dle, cold my fire and grey; By our La - dy's mer - cy, take me in, I pray.

Can you tell the difference between the ♩ and ♩ notes? Can you tell the meaning of *p* and of *f*?

Oct. 25

1. Print the letter-name of each of the following notes.

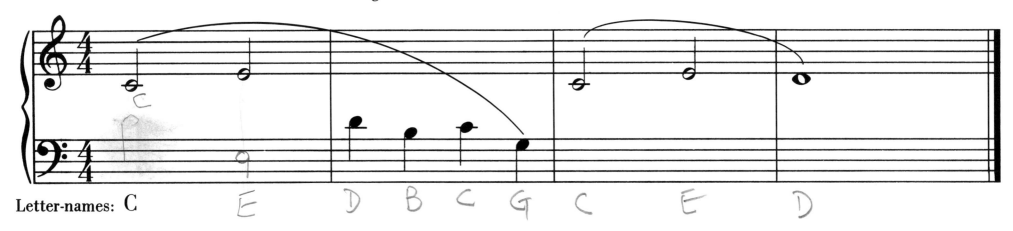

Letter-names: C   E   D   B   C   G   C   E   D

2. Copy the above music.

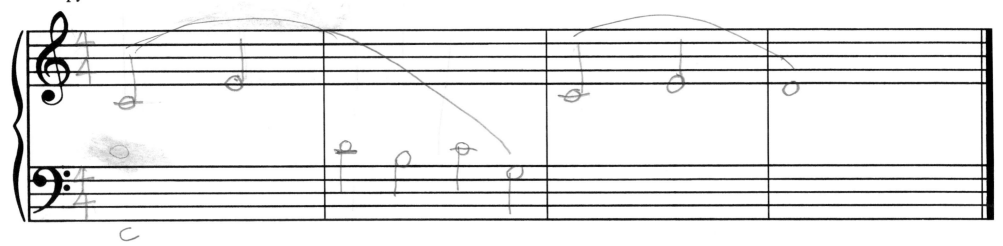

3. Write the time-signature for each measure.

Date ...Oct. 25...........

16th LESSON

D'où viens-tu bergère,
D'où viens-tu?
D'où viens-tu bergère,
D'où viens-tu?

Je viens de la crèche,
Voir l'enfant Jesus;
Sur la paille fraîche
Il est étendu.

Count aloud and clap:

Whence, O Shepherd Maiden?

French-Canadian Carol

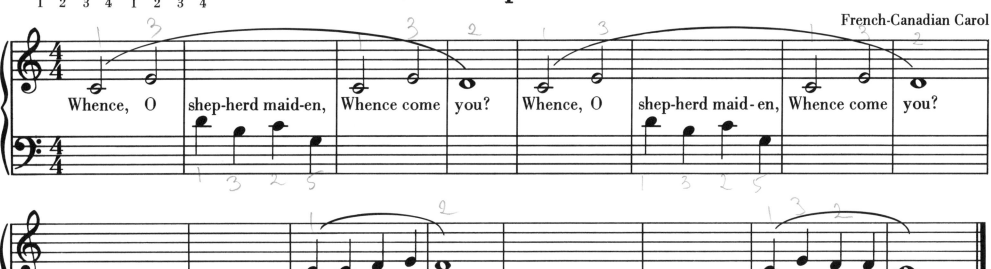

How many phrases does this piece contain?

Oct. 25, Nov 1

— 17th **LESSON IN WRITING** —

1. Print the correct letter-name under each note, then circle each pair of notes forming a skip of a FOURTH.

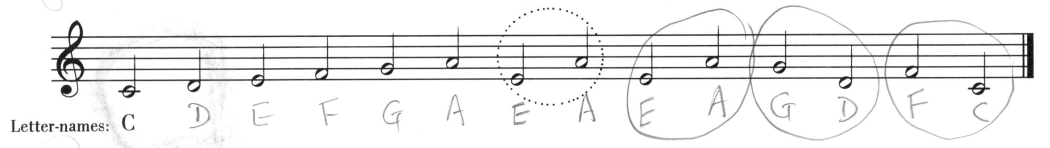

Letter-names: C D E F G A E A E A G D F C

2. Draw a note for each letter-name.

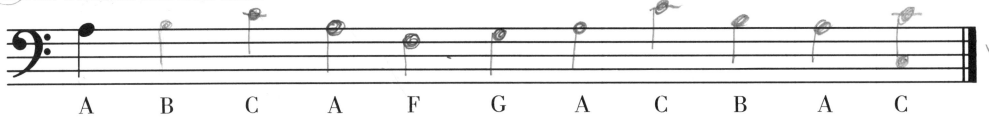

A B C A F G A C B A C

3. Draw bar-lines to divide this tune into measures.

4. Write the time-signature for each measure.

Date ......Oct. 25.........

17th LESSON

Whole
rest

(4-beat rest)

Fingering: 3 2 1 1
left hand   right hand

At the Seashore

Words by Ruth Fraser Cork

f
Here I build my | house of sand: | Ver - y big and | ver - y grand. | I am hav - ing | lots of fun, | Pret - ty soon it | will be done.

p
Soon the waves will | roll up high-er, | Sound-ing like a | might-y show-er. | When my house will | wash a - way, | I'll make one an-oth-er day.

f

There is a NEW NOTE in this lesson. What is it?
Count aloud and clap the notes in this piece.

Oct. 25, Nov 1

1. Write the number of beats (counts) under each rest.

Number
of beats: 2 1 2 4. ├ 4 ├ 1 ├ 1 4

2. Write the counts under each measure.

Count: 1 2 ├ 2 ├ 2 ├ 2 ├ 2 ├ 2 ├ 2

Count: 1 2 3 4 ├ 2 3 4 ├2 3 4 ├ 2 3 4 ├ 2 3 4

3. Draw bar-lines to divide this tune into measures, then write the correct letter-name under each note.

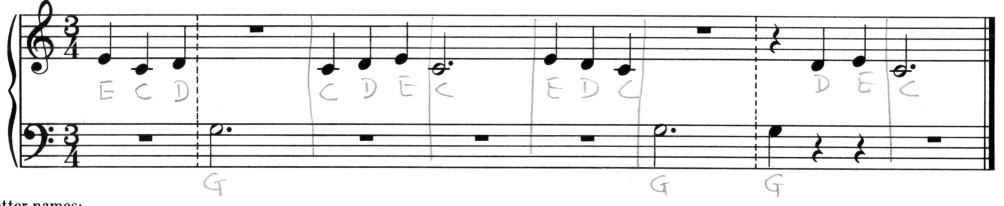

E C D C D E C E D C D E C

G G G

Letter-names:

Date .... *Oct. 25* ....

18th LESSON

Quarter rest
𝄽
(1-beat rest)

Half rest
(2-beat rest)

The Duck

p "Quack, quack, quack!" says the duck. "Quack, quack, quack! Quack, quack, quack!"

Chimes

Count aloud and clap: **3/4** ♩ ♩ ♩ ♩ ♩. ‖
1 2 3 1 2 3

Words by Ruth Fraser Cork

f "Tick, tock, tick, tock!" Says the big clock. Hark to the chime, Tell-ing the time. One, Two, Three.

Remember: The Whole Rest indicates a measure of silence in *any* kind of time.

Nov 1

1. Draw a note for each letter-name.

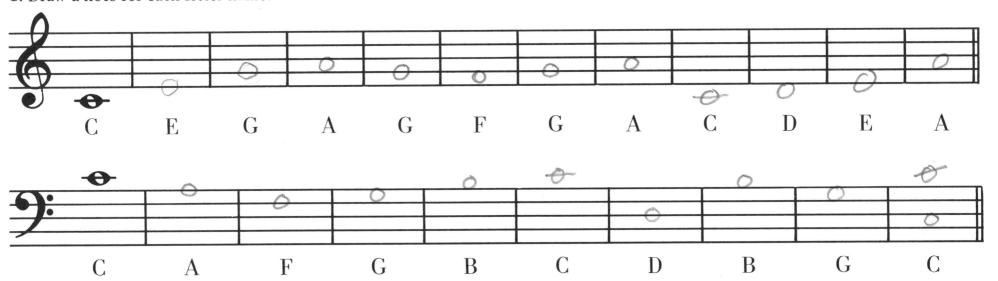

C   E   G   A   G   F   G   A   C   D   E   A

C   A   F   G   B   C   D   B   G   C

2. Draw bar-lines to divide this tune into measures, then write the counts for each measure in the space between the staves.

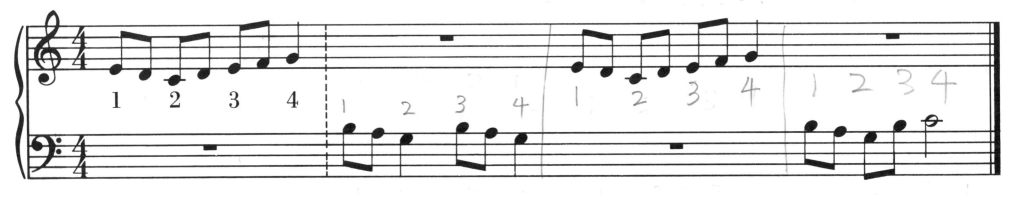

1   2   3   4   1   2   3   4   1   2   3   4   1   2   3   4

3. Write a time-signature for each measure.

Date .... Nov 1, Nov 8

19th LESSON

The Jet Plane

Eighth note
(half beat note)

$\quad \rule{0pt}{0pt}$ = $\rule{0pt}{0pt}$

ff
(fortissimo)
very loud

Count aloud and clap: $\frac{2}{4}$

1 2 1 2

Words by T.R.

p See the jet plane fly - ing in the sun - shine. See the jet-plane fly - ing up so high.

The Pretty Butterflies

Count aloud and clap:

$\frac{4}{4}$

1 2 3 4 1 2 3 4

Words by Ruth Fraser Cork

p See the pret-ty but-ter-flies, Shin-ing bright, in the light. See the hap-py but-ter flies, They're a love-ly sight.

f

ff

Nov 8

1. Complete each measure by adding notes.

2. Draw bar-lines to divide the following into measures.

3. Use an x to mark the correct answer.

p [soft] [loud]   *f* [soft] [loud]   *ff* [very soft] [very loud]   *pp* [very soft] [very loud]

4. Write a time-signature for each measure.

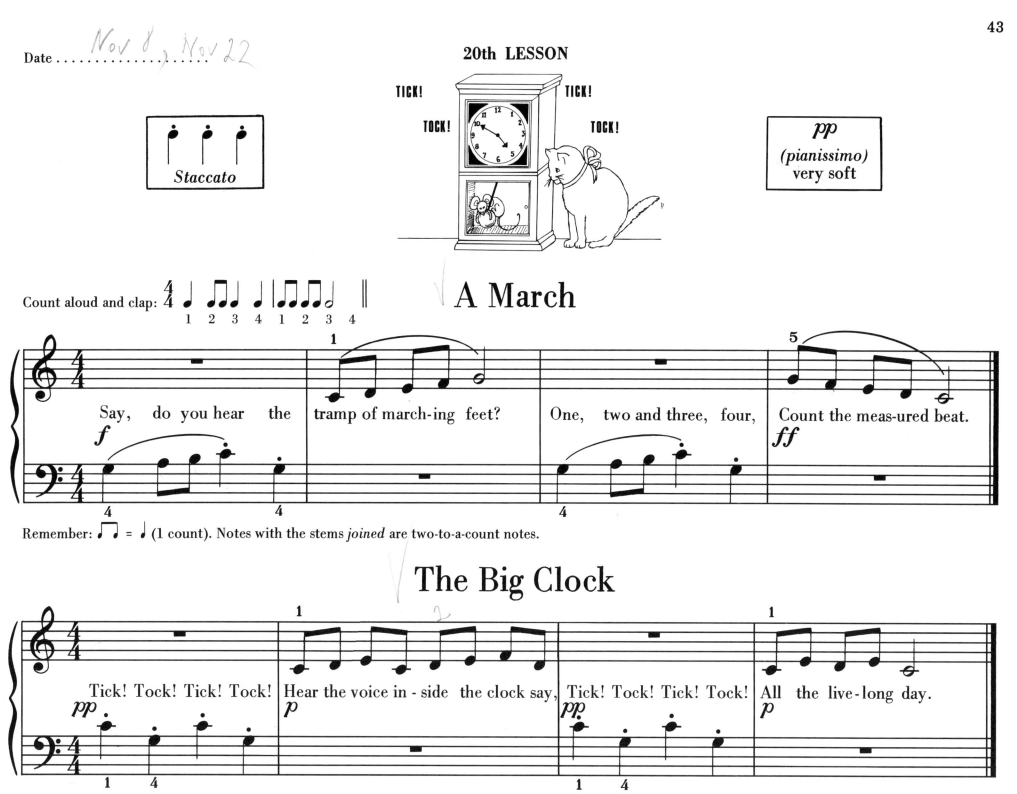

O Canada

arr.
by B.B.

*The 𝅗𝅥. ♪ rhythm can be played by ear.   ** ♯ (Sharp): Play the black key to the right of the note.

The Star-Spangled Banner

New Notes

A B C D E F G

(Pause)
Hold the
note longer
than its full
value.

arr. by B.B.

*The left hand plays in the Treble staff. The ♪. ♬ and ♩. ♪ rhythms can be played by ear.　　**♯ (Sharp): Play the black key to the right of the note.

ELEMENTARY TECHNIC FOR BEGINNERS

(To build the hand and to develop the player's skill and co-ordination)*

Practise hands separately, one hand after the other.

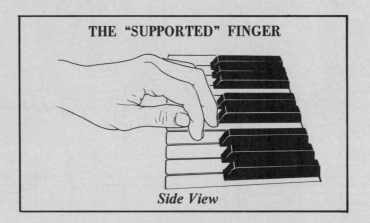

THE "SUPPORTED" FINGER

Side View

Step 1

FOR A GOOD HAND POSITION

1. Support a finger with the thumb (1st finger) by placing the TIP of the thumb against the lower joint (tip) of the finger.

2. Play with the "supported" finger:

1–2 supported finger   1–2   1–3   1–3   1–4   1–4   1–5   1–5

Step 2

FOR FINGER ACTION

1. Support a finger as in Step 1.

2. Play with the supported finger, and, while holding the key down, play the neighbouring key with the next finger:

R.H.

1–2 supported finger   3   3   3   1–3 supported finger   4   4   4   etc.

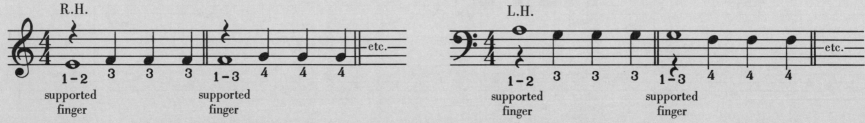

L.H.

1–2 supported finger   3   3   3   1–3 supported finger   4   4   4   etc.

*These exercises may be given to students in connection with their pieces, at the discretion of the teacher.

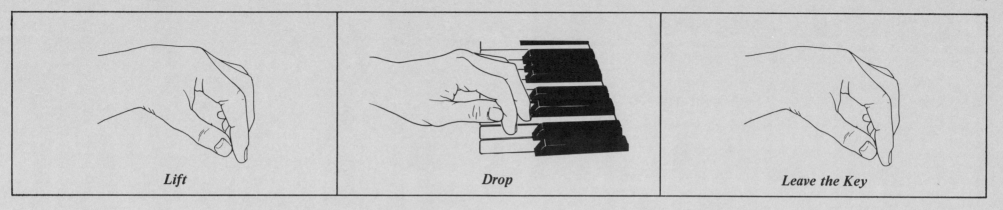

Lift	*Drop*	*Leave the Key*

Step 3 | FOR FLEXIBILITY OF THE WRIST AND A GOOD TONE

1. Support a finger with the thumb, placing the tip of the thumb against the lower joint (tip) of the finger.

2. Slightly LIFT the forearm, letting the hand hang from the wrist above the keyboard.

3. Gently DROP the hand, landing on the key with the tip of the finger. (The finger points to the key.) Let the wrist FOLLOW THROUGH. It will be drawn towards the keyboard, and the weight of the hand will rest on the tip of the supported finger.

4. LEAVE the key by lifting the wrist, which will roll slightly forward, and the forearm. Let the hand hang down in preparation for its drop to the next key.

Example:

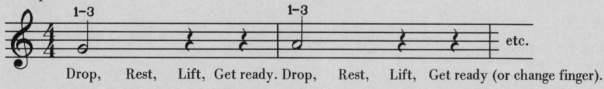

Drop,   Rest,   Lift, Get ready. Drop,   Rest,   Lift, Get ready (or change finger).

Step 4 | FOR PHRASING

1. Let the finger SINK into the first key while the hand and the wrist move downwards.

2. The wrist LIFTS the finger off the last key of each phrase. Start on any white key and play the phrase *legato*. Use fingers 1-2, 2-3, 3-4, 4-5.

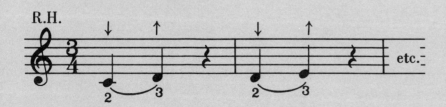

CERTIFICATE

This certifies that

_____

has completed

PART ONE

and is eligible for promotion to

PART TWO

of

The A.B.C. of PIANO PLAYING

_____

Teacher

_____

Date